Gift from the
John Montarula
LITERACY ENDOWMENT FUND

DROPPING IN ON

GRANDMA MOSES

By Pamela Geiger Stephens
Illustrations by Jim McNeill

CrystalProductions
Glenview, Illinois

Library of Congress Cataloging-in-Publication Data

Stephens, Pamela Geiger.
  Dropping in on Grandma Moses / by Pamela Geiger Stephens ; illustrations by Jim McNeill.
     p. cm.
   ISBN 978-1-56290-598-9
  1. Moses, Grandma, 1860-1961—Juvenile literature. I. McNeill, Jim, 1967- II. Title.

  ND237.M78S74 2008
  759.13—dc22
  [B]

                              2008017351

Copyright © 2008 by Crystal Productions Co.

All Rights Reserved

ISBN 978-1-56290-598-9

Printed in Hong Kong

Hello there! My name is Puffer. I am on my way to Eagle Bridge, New York, to visit the famous American artist, Grandma Moses.

Puffer sees a flock of ducks.

"Excuse me," says Puffer to the leader of the ducks. "Is this Eagle Bridge?"

"Quack!" says the duck. (Quack means yes in duck talk.)

"Then this is my stop," Puffer says. "Thanks for your help!"

Puffer tips his hat to thank the duck and loses his balance.

```
W
 H
  O
   A
    A
     A
      A
```

Flutter! Flap! Flap! Flap! Flutter! Flap!

"Look out beeelow!!" Puffer warns. Crash! Bump! Thwack! Thump! Thump! Thump!

Puffer falls from the sky and through a tree. Apples scatter everywhere!

A lady gathering apples nearby is surprised by all the noise. "My goodness! What is all that racket?" she wonders.

Puffer peeps out of a big pile of apples. "Whew! Sorry for the noise, ma'am. I'm afraid that I need some landing lessons."

"I should say so," the lady agrees. "Do you need help getting out of there?"

"No, ma'am, but maybe you could help me find Grandma Moses. She's supposed to live around here."

The lady smiles. "My name is Anna Mary Robertson Moses, but everyone calls me Grandma Moses," she says. "You must be Puffer, the interviewer."

"Yes, ma'am, I am indeed Puffer and I am very pleased to meet you!"

"Well," says Grandma Moses, "as soon as you get out of that pile of apples we can get started with the interview."

Puffer scrambles out of the apples.

"You did a good job getting those apples off the tree," laughs Grandma Moses. "Would you mind picking up a bunch and carrying them to the house for me?"

"I'd be happy to, Grandma Moses!"

Puffer fills his hat with big, red apples. He and Grandma Moses walk to her house.

Puffer is happy when Grandma Moses says, "You can put the apples on the table." The apples are very heavy.

"Now, sit yourself down and let's get to work on your interview," she tells Puffer.

"That would be splendid!"

Puffer takes out his notebook and pencil then asks the first question.

"When did you start painting, Grandma Moses?"

"I took up painting when I was about seventy years old," she replies.

"Seventy years old?! Is that why you are called Grandma Moses?"

Grandma Moses chuckles, "Probably so."

"What sort of paintings did you make?"

"I think it would easier to show you. Would you like to see a painting now?"

"I'd like that very much!"

"The title of this painting is *Sugaring Off in the Maple Orchard*," begins Grandma Moses. "It's about a special time of year when farm neighbors gathered together to make maple syrup."

"Ah ha! Those must be maple trees and the buckets are filled with maple sap!"

"Yes, sir," says Grandma Moses. "We boiled the sap in big kettles to make maple syrup and sugar."

"Was it hard work?"

"Oh, my, yes it was hard work," Grandma Moses exclaims. "But it was also fun. Look closely at the man in the center of the picture. Can you tell what he is doing?"

"He's pouring maple syrup on the snow!"

Grandma Moses smiles, "He's making maple flavored snow ice cream for the children."

"Your painting makes me think that some farm chores could be yummy."

"Yes indeed!" agrees Grandma Moses.

"Growing up on a farm must have given you some good memories, Grandma Moses."

"Yes, it did," answers Grandma Moses.

"Did you always live on a farm?"

"Yes, sir!" Grandma Moses proudly says. "I was born and raised on a farm.

"My parents had a farm in upstate New York. I was born there in 1860. I had five brothers and four sisters."

"Were your parents artists?"

"Oh, no, but my father helped me to draw," answers Grandma Moses.

"Sometimes when my father went to the store he would buy paper and chalk for me," Grandma Moses explains.

"That was a real treat. It was even better than candy to me because it lasted longer."

"What did you like to draw when you were a little girl?"

Grandma Moses thinks for a moment, then replies, "I liked to draw what I thought was called lambscapes…

"I was much older before I found out that pictures about the outdoors were called landscapes!"

Puffer and Grandma Moses laugh together at her funny story.

"When I was still a young girl I became a housekeeper on a nearby farm. I worked there for a long time," says Grandma Moses.

"One day, a very handsome young man named Thomas was hired at the same farm," Grandma Moses adds.

"Before too long, Thomas and I married…

…and we moved to a farm in Virginia," explains Grandma Moses.

"I have an idea, Puffer," says Grandma Moses.

"Since we are talking about moving from one farm to another, would you like to see a painting that I call *Moving Day on the Farm*?" she asks.

"Yes, please! I'd like that a lot!"

Grandma Moses begins to tell about the painting. "A long time ago, moving day was a time for friends and neighbors to get together."

Puffer looks at the painting. "That must be why there are so many people in the painting!"

"Oh, yes," Grandma Moses answers. "Little kids, big kids, and grown-ups would all help. Do you see the little girl holding the reins for the horse and some boys holding baskets?"

Puffer answers, "The little girl must be helping with the animals and the little boys must have been moving baskets and barrels."

"You are right," says Grandma Moses. "I'm sure you also see many grown-ups working and visiting with each other in the picture."

Puffer finds the grown-ups in the painting. "It looks as if the grown-ups are moving the heavy things and loading the wagons."

"Moving day was hard work," adds Grandma Moses. "But having friends to help made it much easier."

"I like the way you tell stories with your artwork, Grandma Moses. Would you tell me how you make your paintings?"

"Maybe it would be more fun if you tried to make a painting yourself," she replies.

"I'd like that very much!"

"First, you need to think about a story that you want to tell," Grandma Moses tells Puffer.

Puffer has an idea. He is going to tell the story of meeting Grandma Moses and gathering apples.

"First, I like to find pictures in magazines or newspapers to help tell my stories," Grandma Moses explains.

"You will need something to paint on, a pencil, some paint, and brushes," says Grandma Moses.

Puffer gathers the magazine pictures and the supplies.

"I'm ready!"

"Now practice placing the pictures on the page until they are in just the right spot," instructs Grandma Moses.

"Next, trace over the pictures. Trace only the main parts, not the details," she adds.

"It's time to add a background."

"You can draw hills, clouds, people, or just about anything," suggests Grandma Moses.

"Use your paint and brushes to add colors and details," Grandma Moses says. "If you don't have a brush, you can always use a twig or a cotton swab."

Puffer is pleased with his painting. "Thank you for helping me learn how to tell a story with a painting, Grandma Moses."

Grandma Moses smiles, "You are very welcome, Puffer."

"I have an idea," says Grandma Moses. "Now that you know how paintings can tell stories, let's see if you can figure out the story in another painting."

"Okay. I'll give it a try."

"This painting tells the story of a fun holiday," Grandma Moses explains as she shows a painting to Puffer. "What do you see?"

Puffer rubs his chin as he thinks. "I see something spooky."

"Spooky?" Grandma Moses asks. "What's so spooky about this picture?"

"The gray color of the sky, the clouds over the moon, and the houses in the background all make the painting seem a little bit spooky. I also see children in costumes, and on the lawn, there are jack-o-lanterns. I think the painting must be telling about Hallowe'en."

"You are right, Puffer, and *Hallowe'en* is the title of the painting, too!" laughs Grandma Moses.

"Hallowe'en must have been a fun time for you."

"Oh, my goodness, yes!" exclaims Grandma Moses. "Hallowe'en was a fun day for us all."

Puffer enjoys learning about the stories that the paintings of Grandma Moses tell, but he is ready to hear more about her life. "What happened after you and Thomas moved to Virginia?"

Grandma Moses replies, "We lived in Virginia for quite a while, but Thomas was always homesick for Eagle Bridge.

"We finally packed our belongings and moved our family of five children back to New York."

"When we moved into our farm home in Eagle Bridge, I wallpapered the rooms and made our house a little fancier.

"One of my paintings was a landscape that I painted to go in front of the fireplace when it wasn't being used.

"Everyone seemed to like my painting on the fireboard. After that, I tried to paint as much as I could."

"After a while, I had enough paintings to enter in a local fair. I also brought along my fruit preserves."

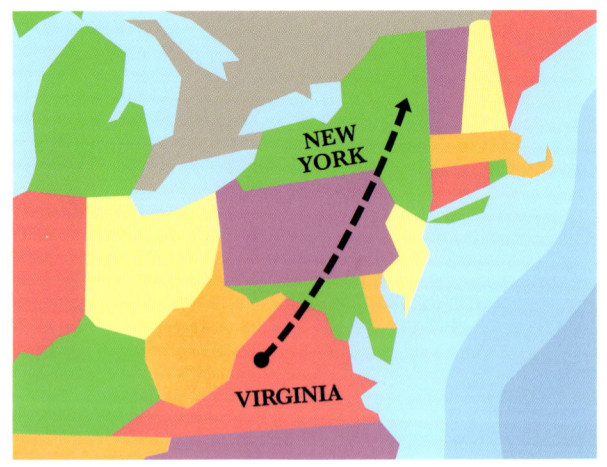

"Did your artwork win any prizes, Grandma Moses?"

Grandma Moses replies, "Well, the paintings didn't win any awards …

… but everyone loved my preserves!"

"Later, a drugstore in a little town nearby let me put my paintings in their windows," says Grandma Moses.

"One day, Mister Louis Caldor passed by the drugstore where he saw my paintings in the window," Grandma Moses continues.

"Mister Caldor liked my paintings so much that he bought them all!" exclaims Grandma Moses.

"Mister Caldor told me that I was going to be a famous artist, and he was right.

"Before too long there were Grandma Moses greeting cards, Grandma Moses fabrics, and Grandma Moses plates," she tells Puffer.

"One time I was even asked to make a painting for the President of the United States!"

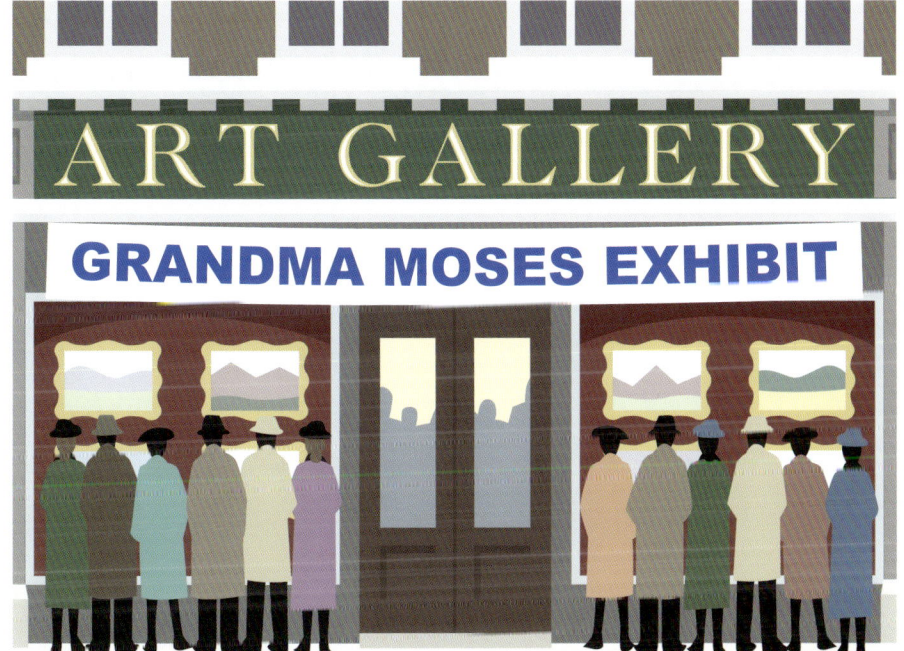

"My paintings were in art shows in New York, Europe, and Japan. It seems as if everyone liked my artwork," says Grandma Moses.

"Does your kind of artwork have a name, Grandma Moses?"

"It is usually called folk art," answers Grandma Moses.

"Why is that?"

"That's because I never went to art school and many of my paintings are about everyday sorts of events."

"Ahh, I understand."

"Would you like to see another painting?" Grandma Moses asks.

"Yes, please!"

Grandma Moses shows Puffer a painting and says, "The title of this painting is *Taking in Laundry*. Do you see why it might be called folk art?" she asks.

"Yes, ma'am, I do indeed! The painting is about your memory of an everyday event."

"Right you are, Puffer," answers Grandma Moses. "When I was younger, doing laundry was a big job that could take all day. We didn't have fancy washing machines or clothes dryers. Laundry was washed in scrub buckets and hung on a line to dry. You also can see what happens when a surprise storm comes," says Grandma Moses.

Puffer looks closely at the painting. "It looks as if people have to rush to take in the clean clothes."

"That is a fact!" exclaims Grandma Moses.

Puffer looks at his notes. "I wonder, Grandma Moses, do all of your paintings show the outdoors?"

"Not all of my paintings are landscapes. Some show the indoors," Grandma Moses replies.

"Could I see a painting that shows an indoor scene?"

"Certainly!" says Grandma Moses.

"I call this painting *The Quilting Bee*. Do you know what a quilting bee is, Puffer?" asks Grandma Moses.

"Sure! It's when a group of people get together to make a quilt. The eight ladies in the background are sewing together a patchwork quilt."

"Quilting bees were also a time to get together for fun. It was like a party," Grandma Moses says.

"That must be why there are so many people in the house. All the food on the table looks yummmeeee!"

"You are exactly right," replies Grandma Moses.

"I think I see something else that is important in this painting, Grandma Moses."

"What's that?" she asks.

"This painting is an indoor scene, but you've also shown a landscape through the windows."

"That's because landscapes are my favorite thing to paint," answers Grandma Moses. "Would you like to see one more painting?"

"Yes, ma'am, I'd like that a lot!"

"This painting shows the story of a special celebration. Can you tell what it is?" asks Grandma Moses.

"It looks like some sort of fancy party."

Grandma Moses tells Puffer, "Look a little closer. The clothes the people are wearing should give you a clue about the celebration."

Puffer looks closely at the painting. "I see! It's a wedding!"

"Yes, indeed! The title of the painting is *A Country Wedding*. Country weddings were just like weddings today. They were a reason to dress up and celebrate!"

"I am a little confused, Grandma Moses. Why there are so many brides and grooms?"

"I've been asked that many times," says Grandma Moses. Then she asks, "Why do *you* think there are so many brides and grooms?"

"Could it be that each part of the painting is telling a different part of the same story?"

"That could be," replies Grandma Moses. "That could be."

Bong! Bong! Bong! Bong! Bong!

A clock loudly chimes and startles Puffer.

"It's getting late. I should be on my way."

"I'm glad you could drop in, Puffer," says Grandma Moses. "Come back anytime."

"Thank you for showing your artwork to me."

Puffer waves good-bye to Grandma Moses and gets ready to fly away.

I hope that you had a good time learning about Grandma Moses and her artwork.

The next time you visit an art museum, look for paintings by Grandma Moses. Try to figure out what story the paintings tell.

Until I see you again, good-bye!!!

GLOSSARY

Caldor, Louis Art collector who discovered Grandma Moses' artwork in Hoosick Falls, New York

Eagle Bridge Village in upstate New York where Grandma Moses lived much of her life and the setting for many of her works of art

Folk Art Artwork usually made by self-trained artists or by artists with not much formal art training

Galerie St. Etienne New York gallery where Grandma Moses had her first one-woman exhibition

Grandma Moses (1860-1961) Anna Mary Robertson Moses, a well-known American folk artist who began her professional career late in life and became one of the most beloved artists of the 20th century. She is known for artwork that shows her memories of everyday life, seasons, and farm chores

Preserves Fruits that are prepared by cooking and sealed in jars to prevent spoilage

---

Image Credits

Sugaring Off in Maple Orchard
1940. Oil on canvas, 18½ x 24½ inches
Private Collection
© 2008 Grandma Moses Properties Co., NY

Moving Day on the Farm
1951. Oil on pressed wood, 17 x 22 inches
Private Collection
© 2008 Grandma Moses Properties Co., NY

Hallowe'en
1955. Oil on pressed wood, 18 x 24 inches
Private Collection
© 2008 Grandma Moses Properties Co., NY

Taking in Laundry
1951. Oil on pressed wood, 17 x 21¾ inches
Private Collection
© 2008 Grandma Moses Properties Co., NY

Quilting Bee
1950. Oil on pressed wood, 20 x 24 inches
Private Collection
© 2008 Grandma Moses Properties Co., NY

A Country Wedding
1951. Oil on pressed wood, 17 x 21¾ inches
The Bennington Museum, Bennington, VT
© 2008 Grandma Moses Properties Co., NY